Popular Performer

Arranged by BERT KONOWITZ

The Best Songs from Broadway, Movies and Radio of the 1940s

The 1940s has left us with a stunning array of memorable and moving music. This volume revisits those songs, casting them in the rich voice of the piano. Standards that originated in Broadway musicals are represented such as "Come Rain or Come Shine" from *St. Louis Woman* (1946) and "How about You" from *Babes on Broadway* (1941). There are also songs from the silver screen such as "Laura" from *Laura* (1944) and "Moonlight in Vermont" from *Moonlight in Vermont* (1943). The jaunty swing of "You Make Me Feel So Young," the tender phrases of "You'll Never Know," and all the other wonderful musical moments are certain to provide hours of enjoyment for the pianist who wishes to be a *Popular Performer*.

CONTENTS

Alfred

At Last

Lyrics by Mack Gordon
Music by Harry Warren
Arr. Bert Konowitz

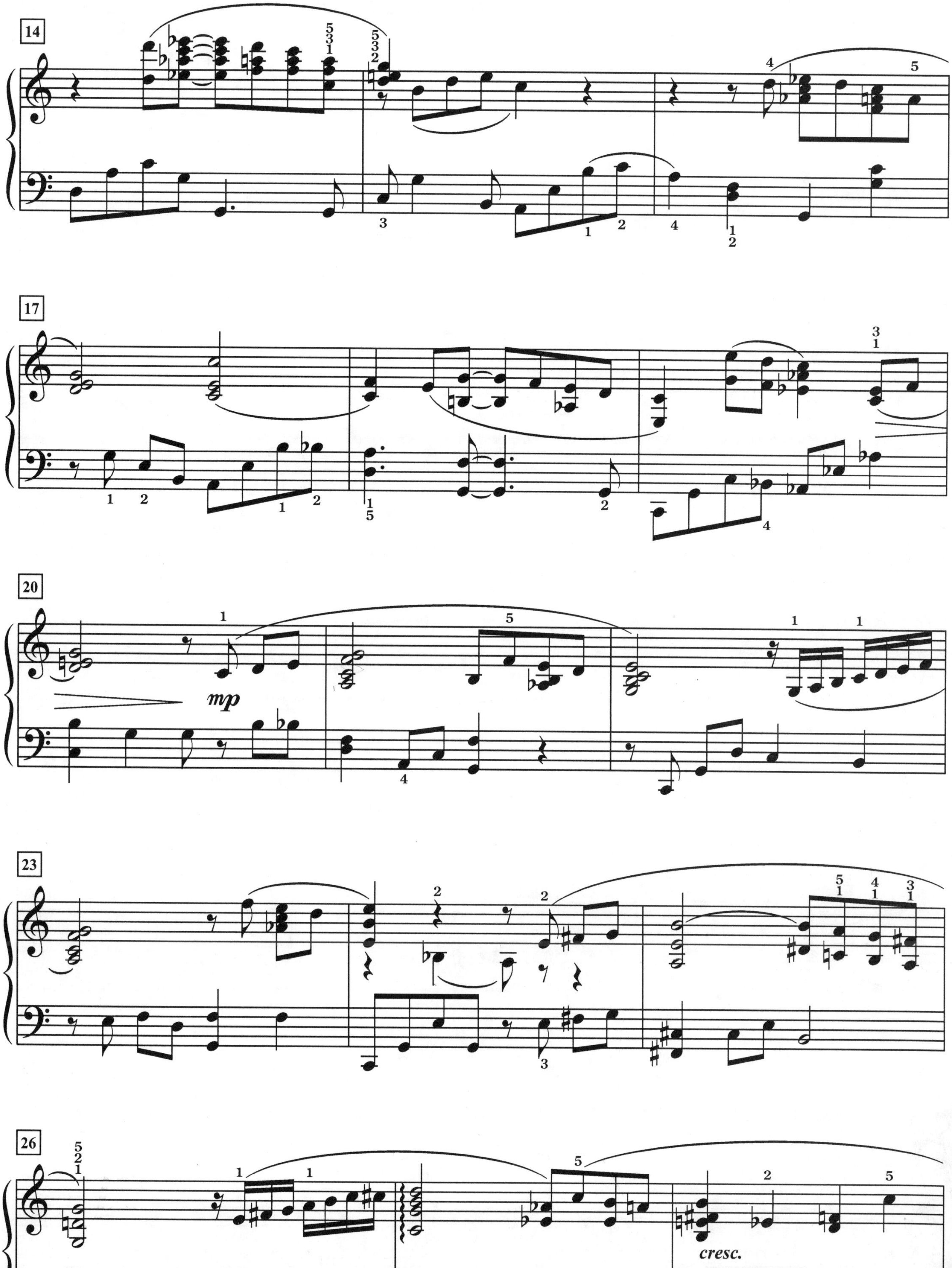
14
17
20
mp
23
26
cresc.

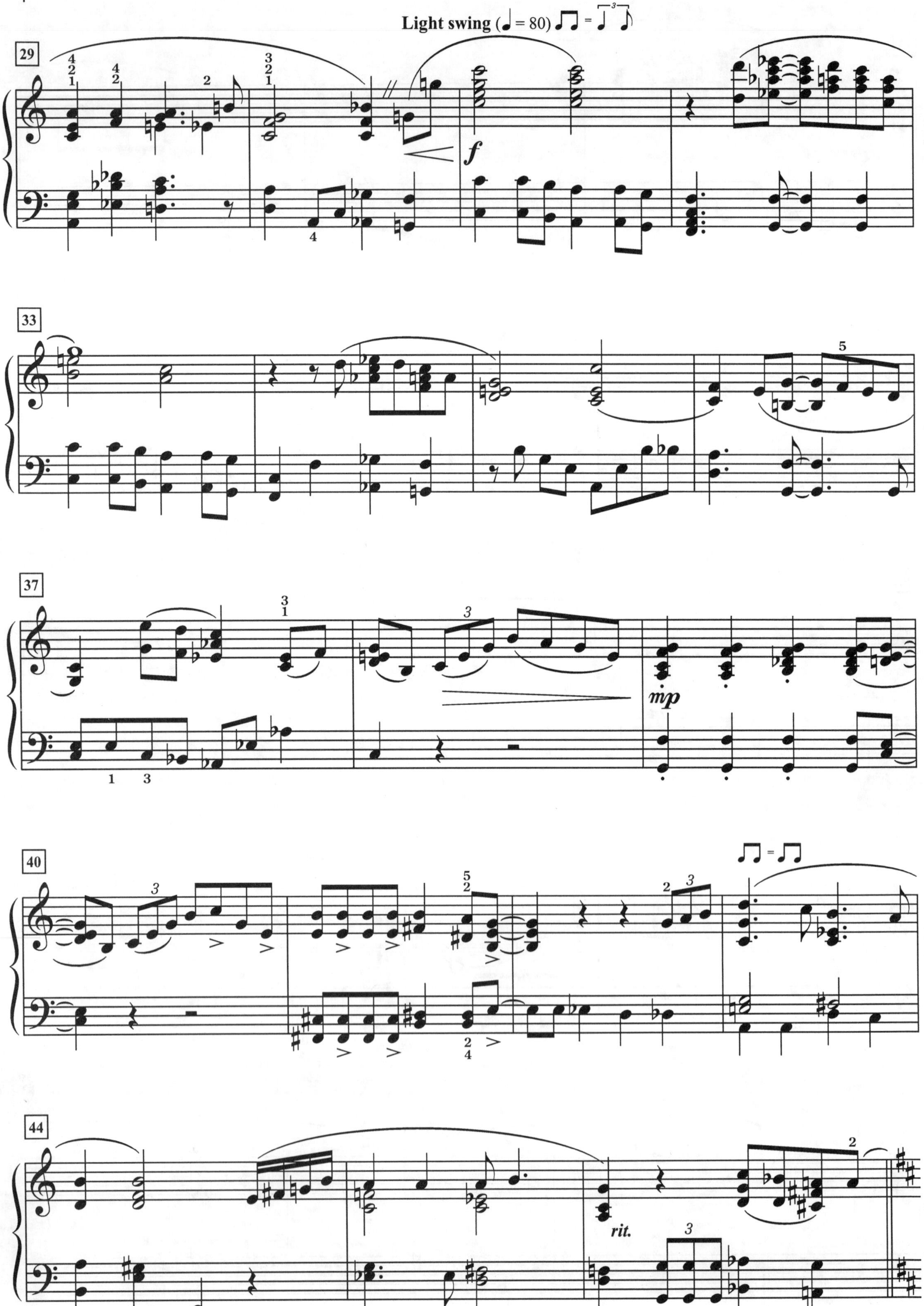
Light swing (♩ = 80)
29
f
33
37
mp
40
44
rit.

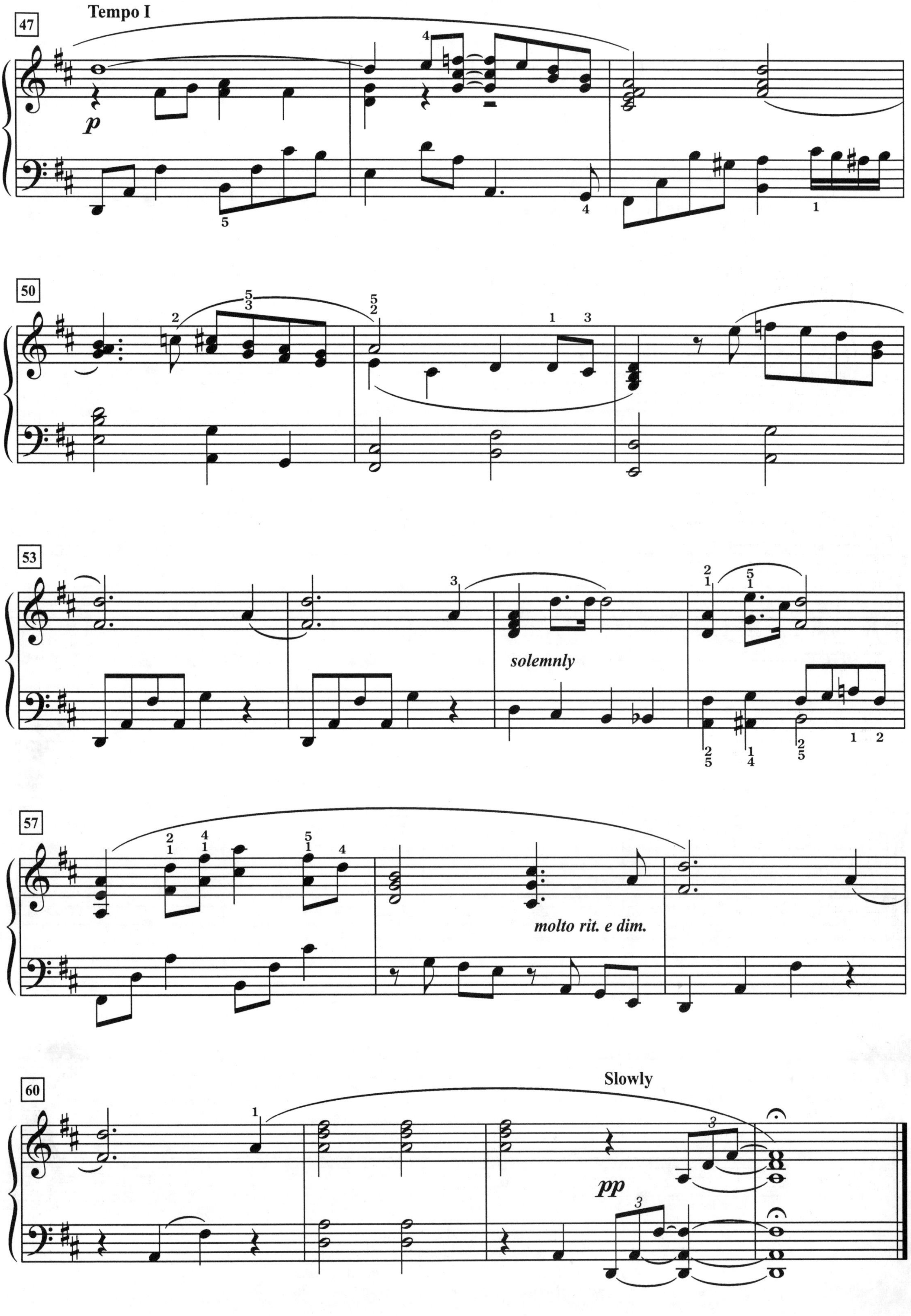
47
Tempo I
p
50
53
solemnly
57
molto rit. e dim.
60
Slowly
pp

Come Rain or Come Shine

Lyrics by Johnny Mercer
Music by Harold Arlen
Arr. Bert Konowitz

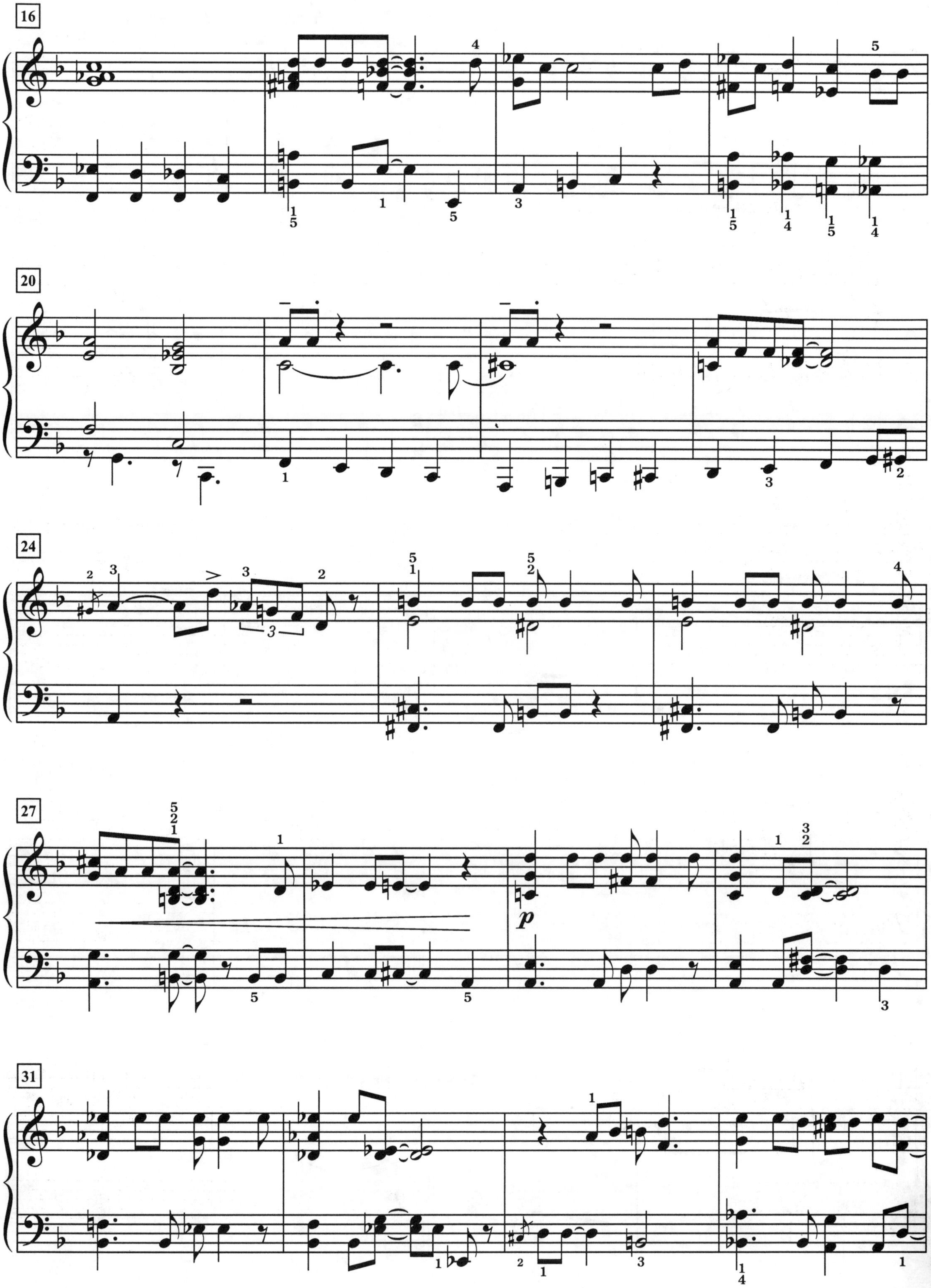
16
20
24
27
31
p

8

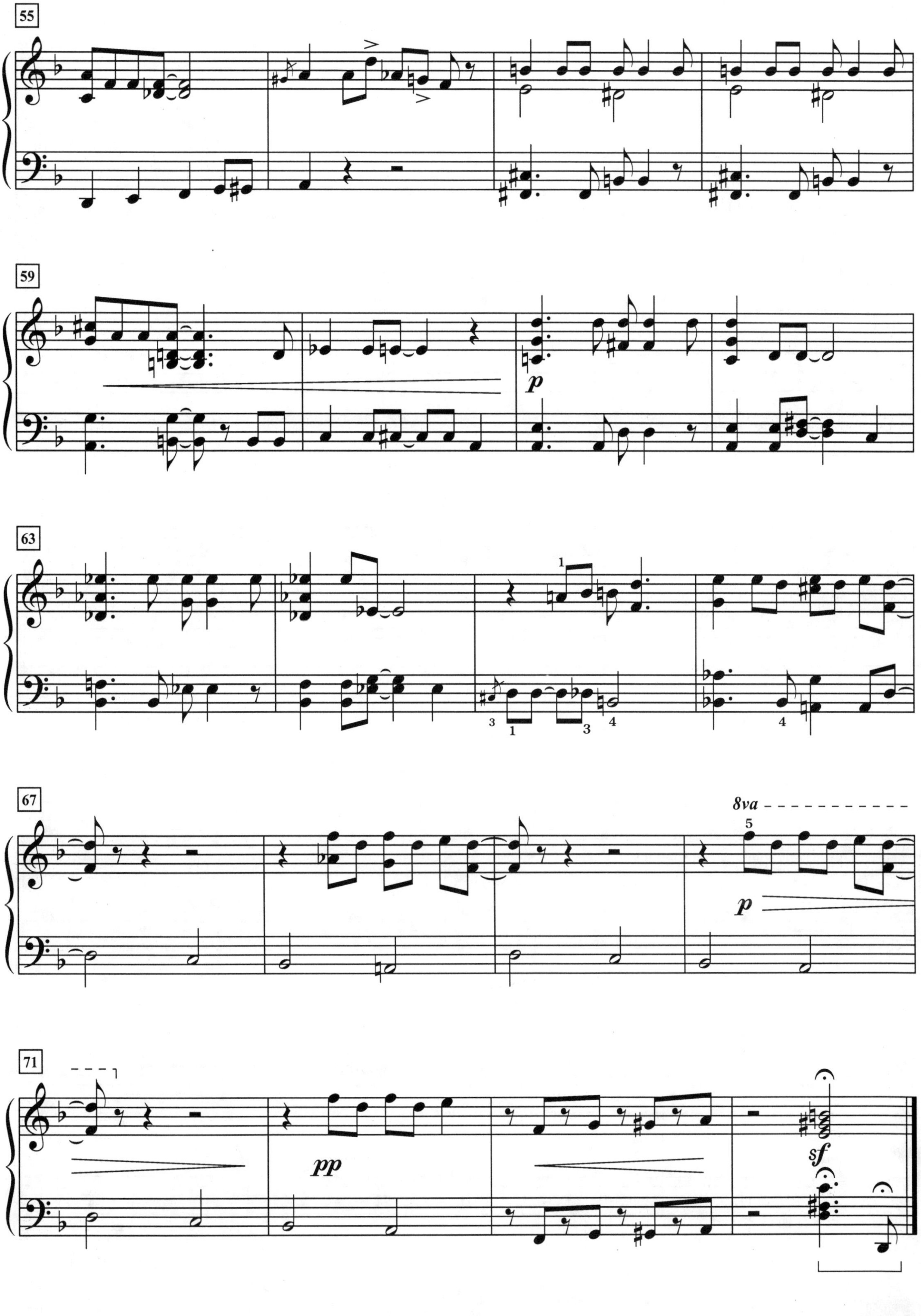
55
59
p
63
67
8va
p
71
pp
sf

How About You

Music by Burton Lane
Words by Ralph Freed
Arr. Bert Konowitz

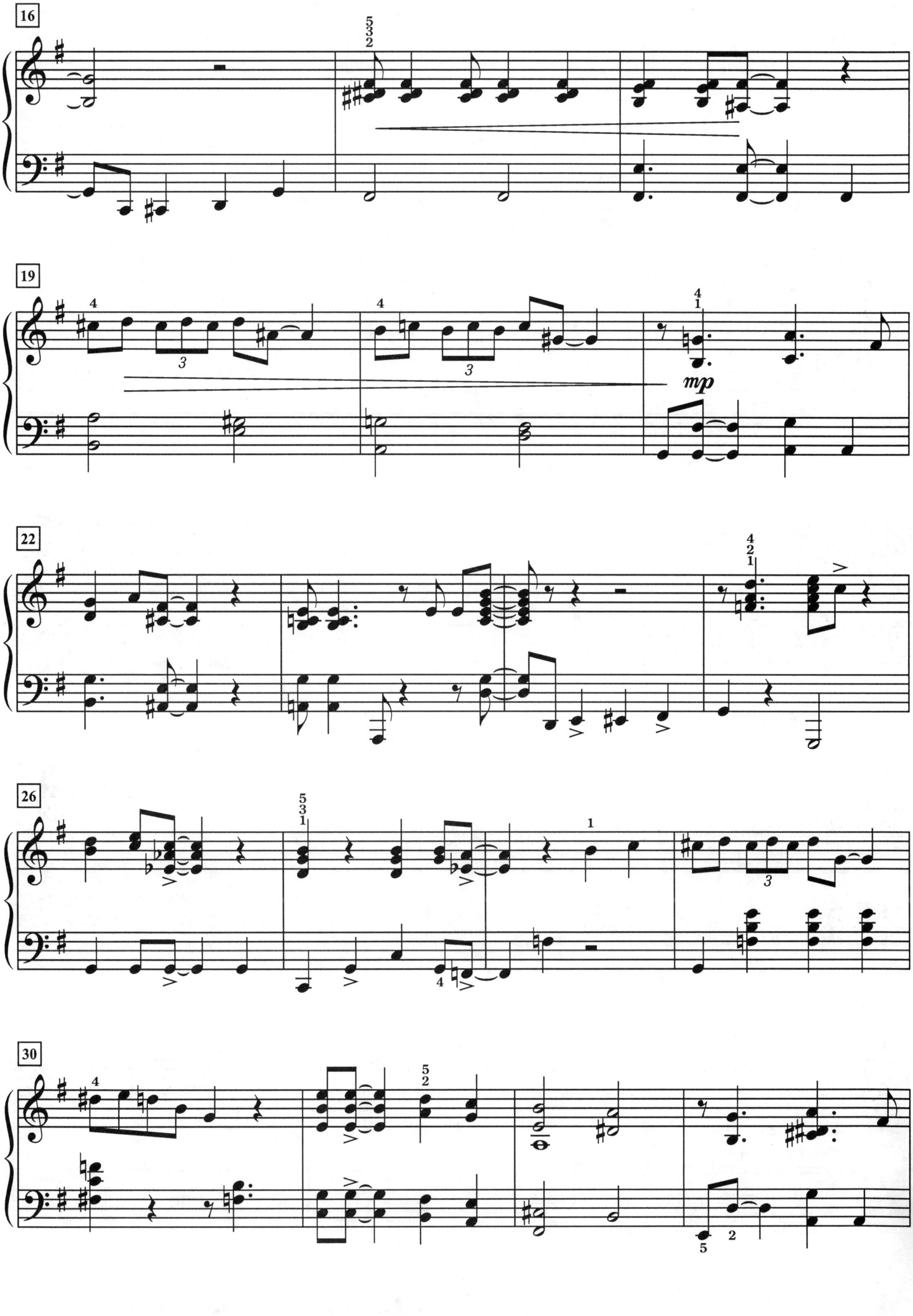
16
19
mp
22
26
30

(LH solo, like a bass player)

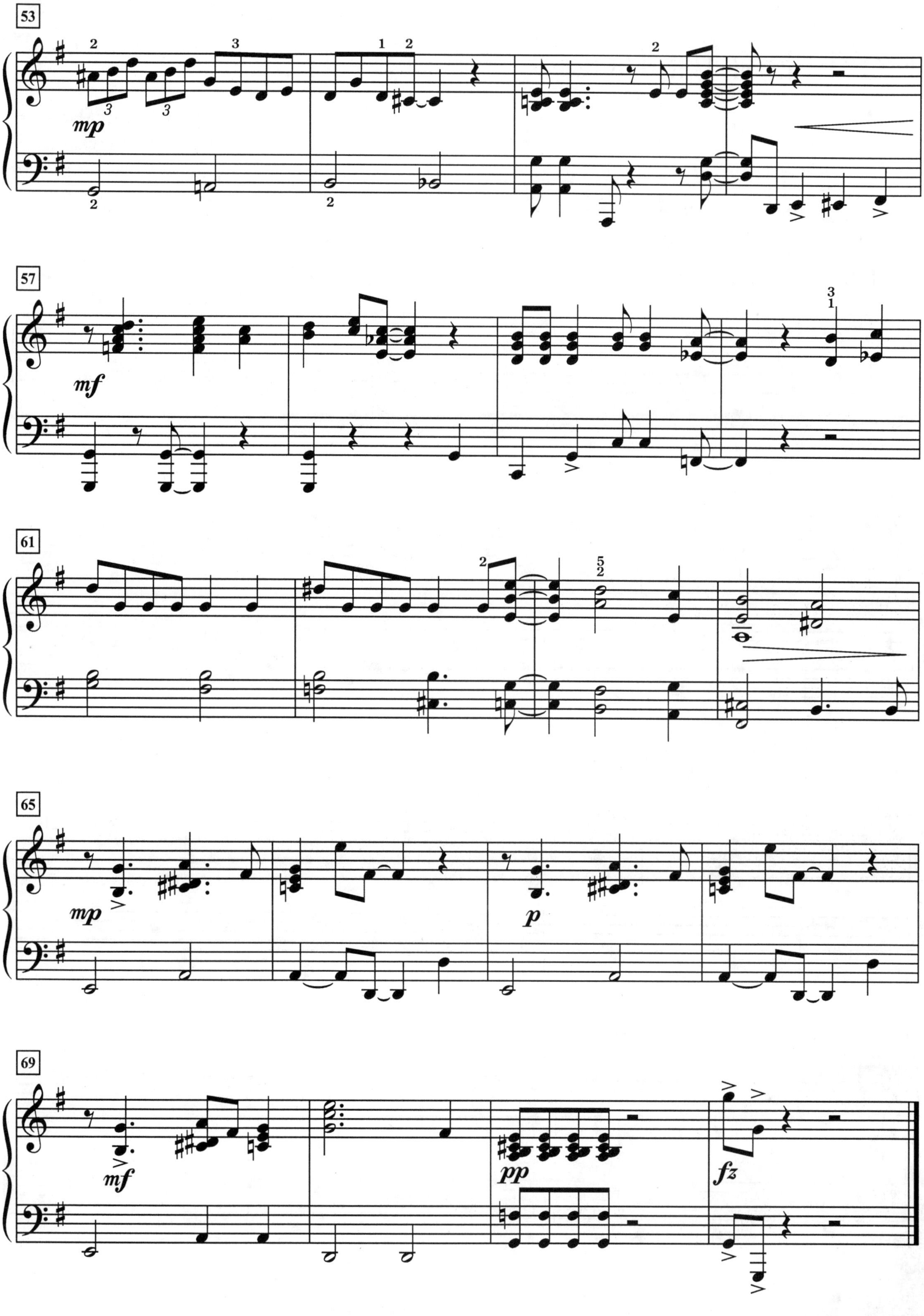
53
mp
57
mf
61
65
mp
p
69
mf
pp
fz

How High the Moon

Lyrics by Nancy Hamilton
Music by Morgan Lewis
Arr. Bert Konowitz

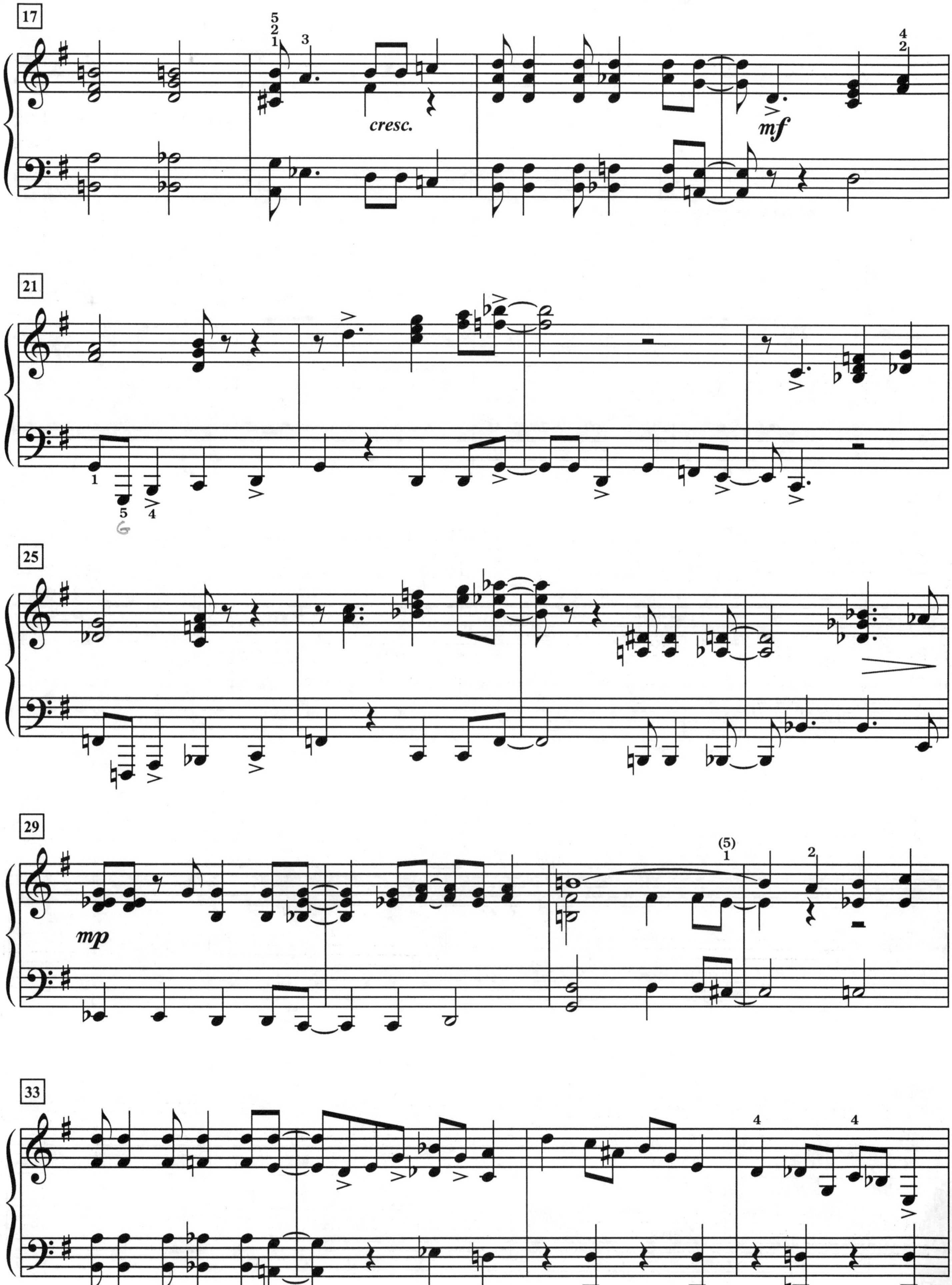
17
cresc.
mf
21
25
29
mp
33

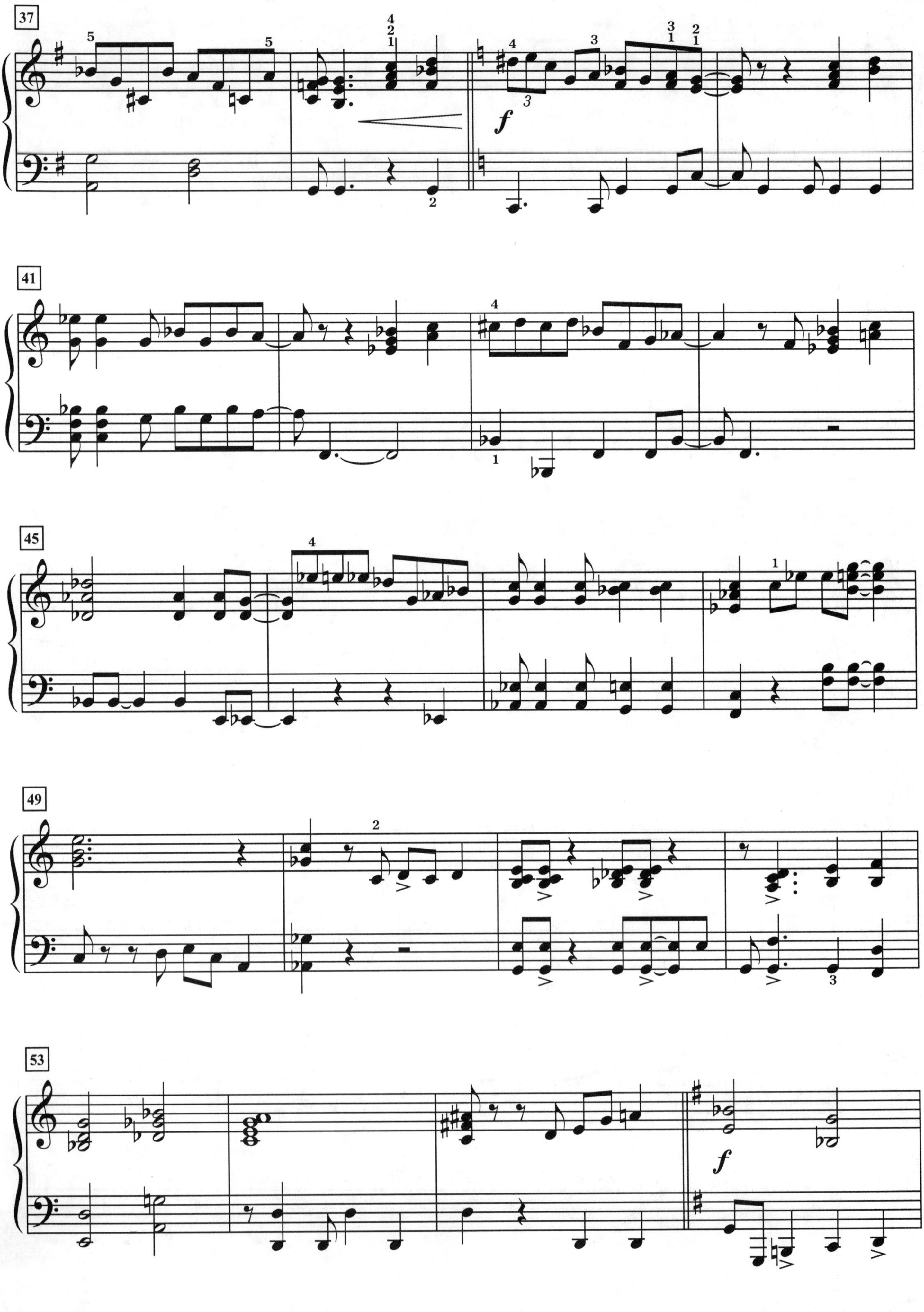
37
f
41
45
49
53
f

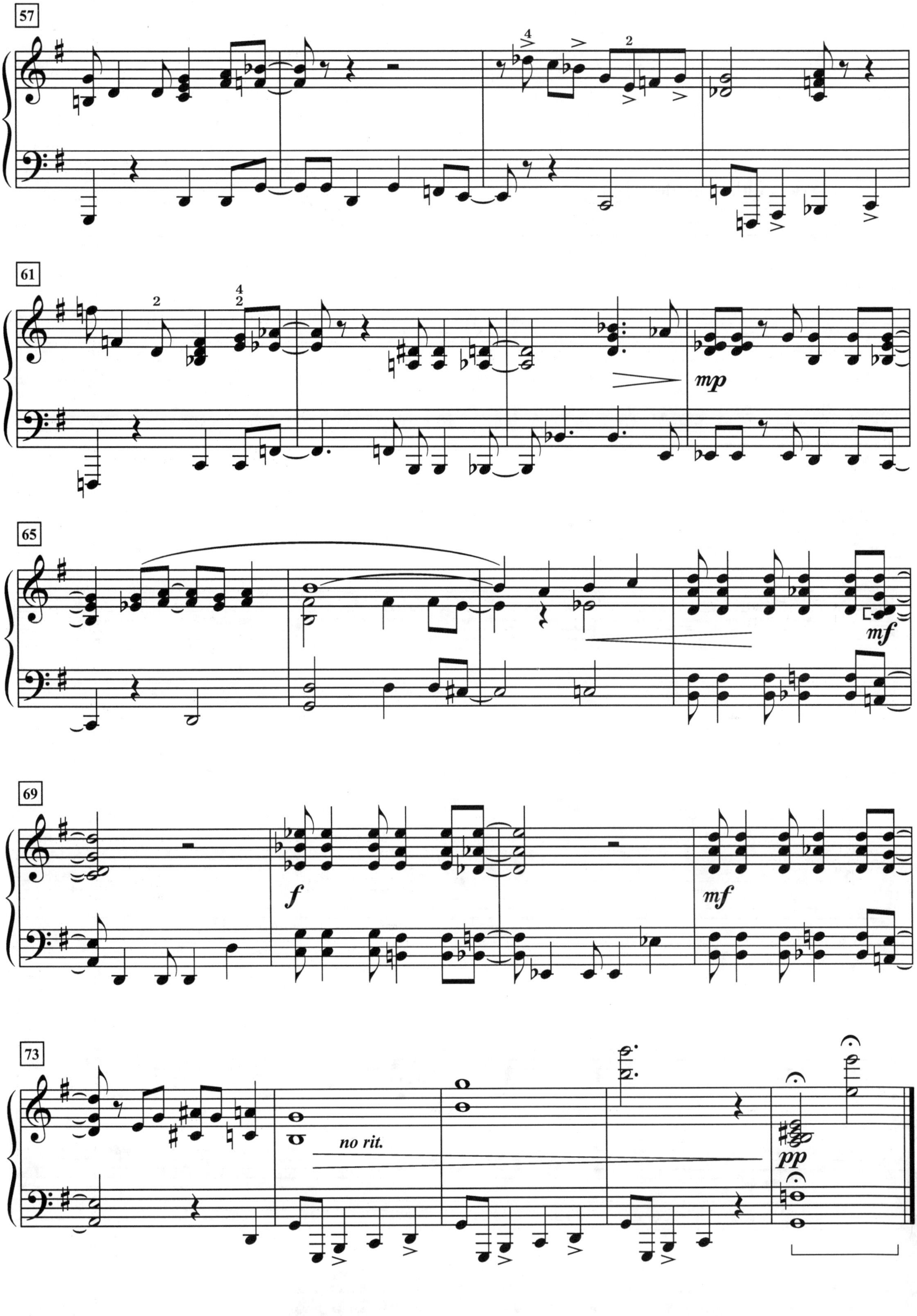
57
61
mp
65
mf
69
f
mf
73
no rit.
pp

Laura

Lyric by Johnny Mercer
Music by David Raksin
Arr. Bert Konowitz

Freely with expression ($\half = 52$)

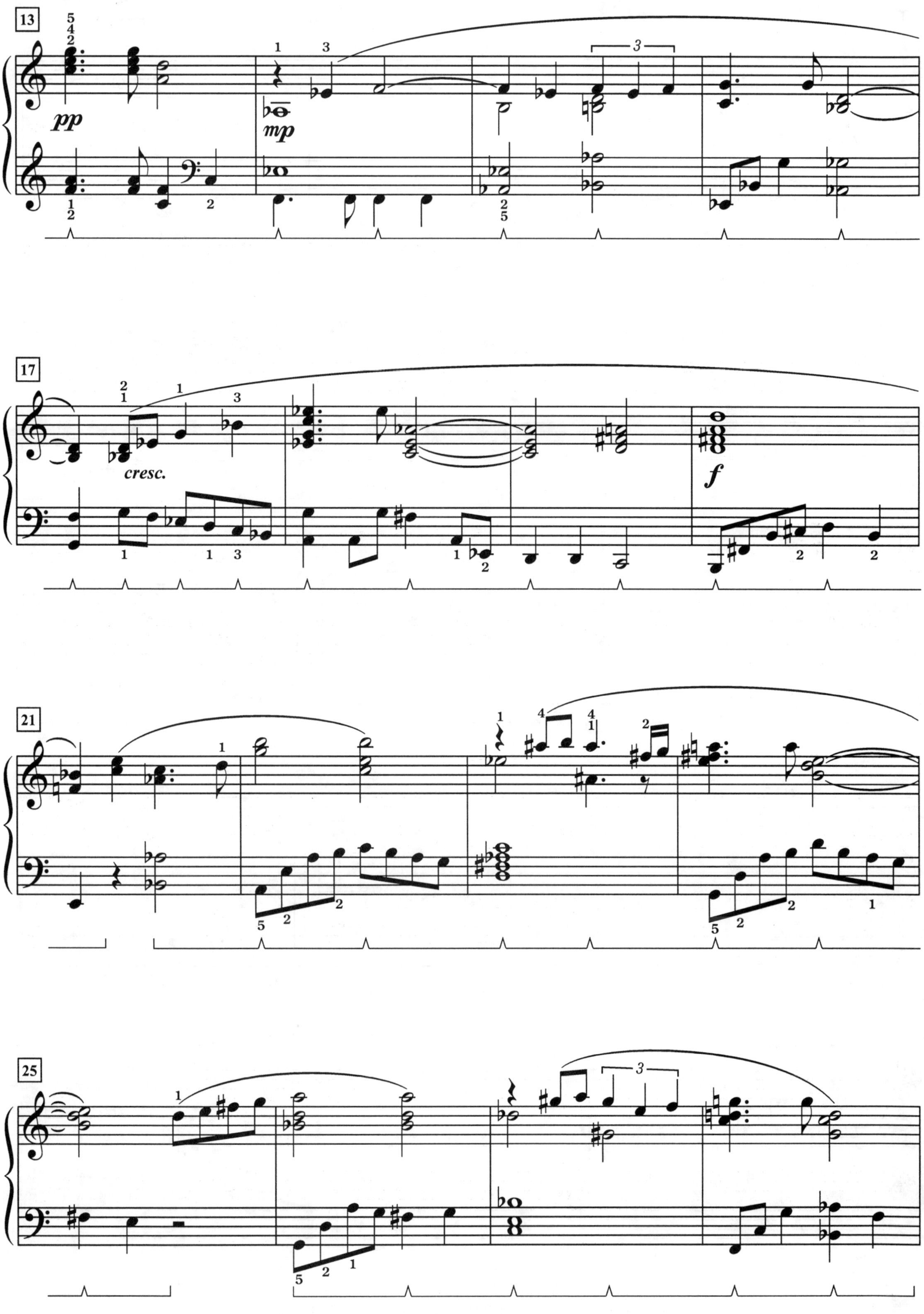
13
pp
mp
17
cresc.
f
21
25

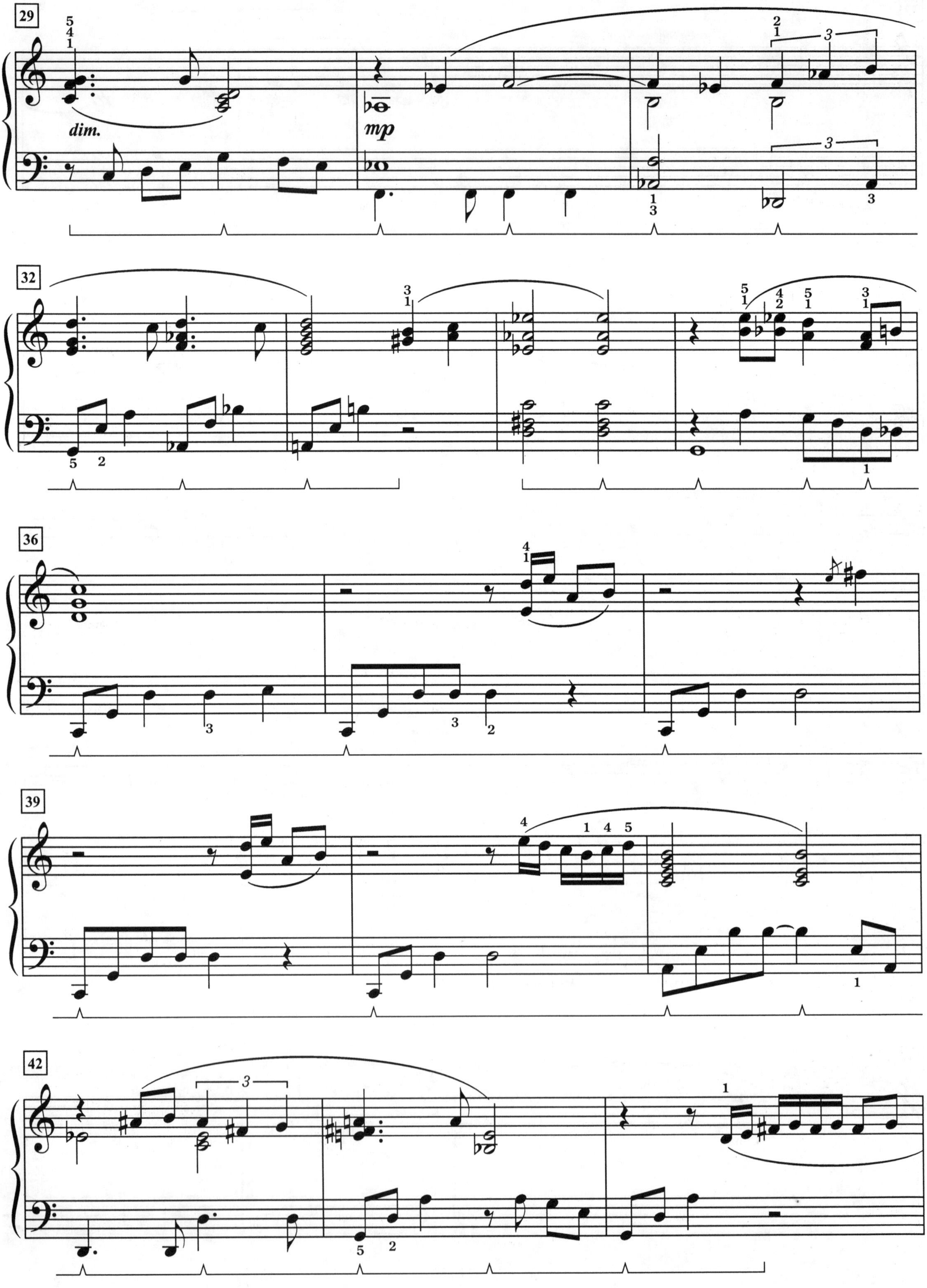
29
dim.
mp
32
36
39
42

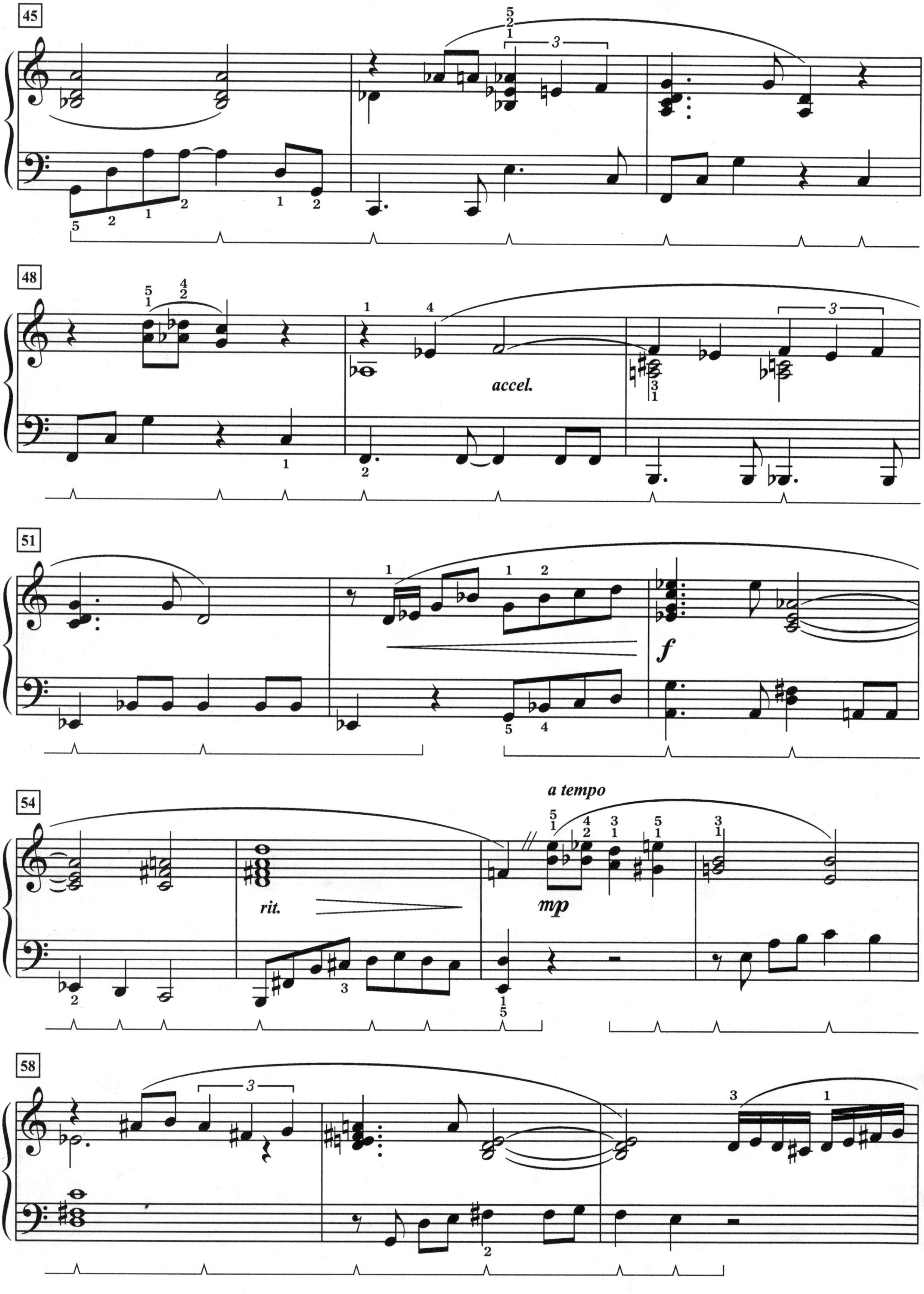
45
48
accel.
51
f
54
rit.
a tempo
mp
58

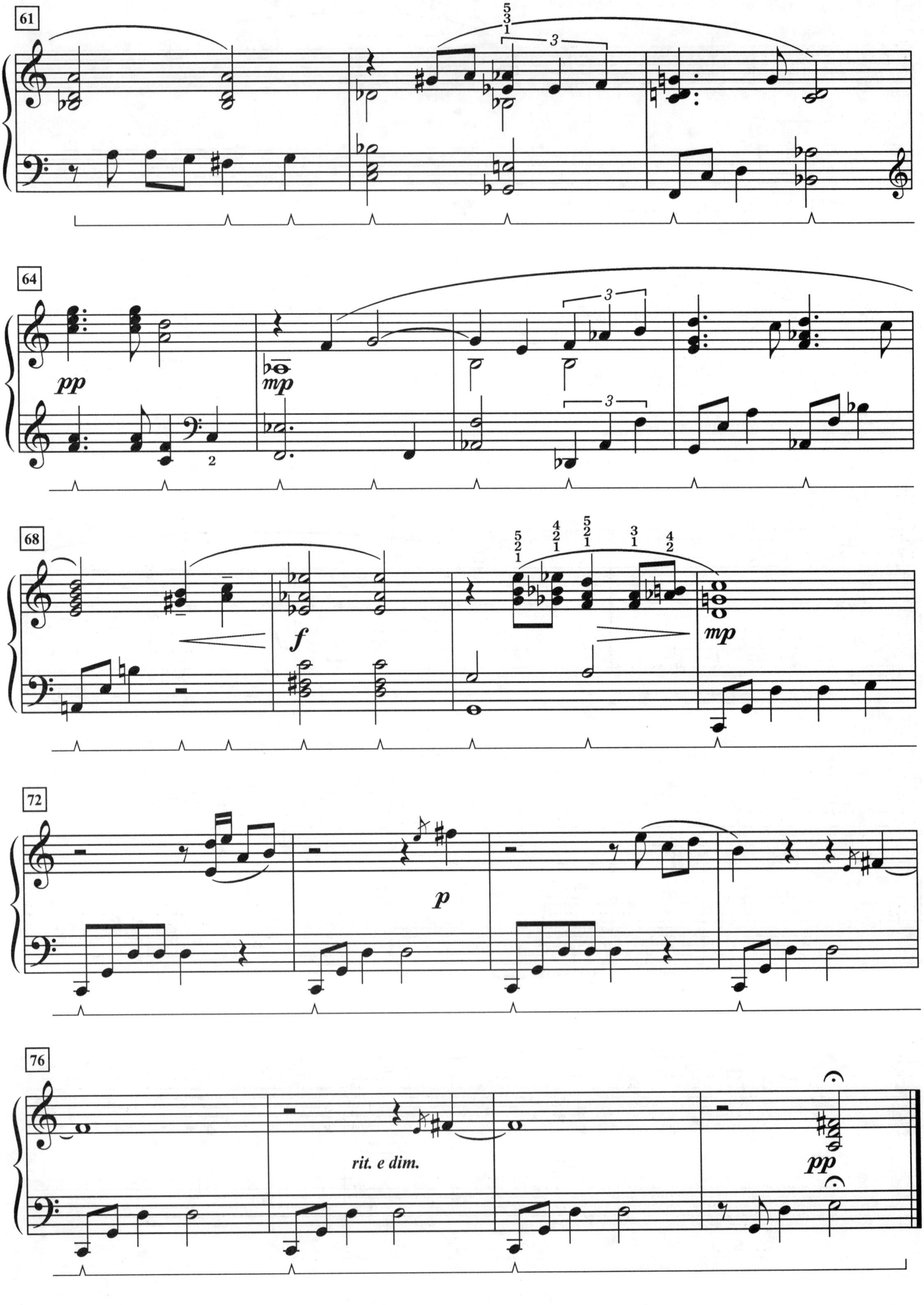
61
64
pp
mp
68
f
mp
72
p
76
rit. e dim.
pp

You Make Me Feel So Young

Words by Mack Gordon
Music by Josef Myrow
Arr. Bert Konowitz

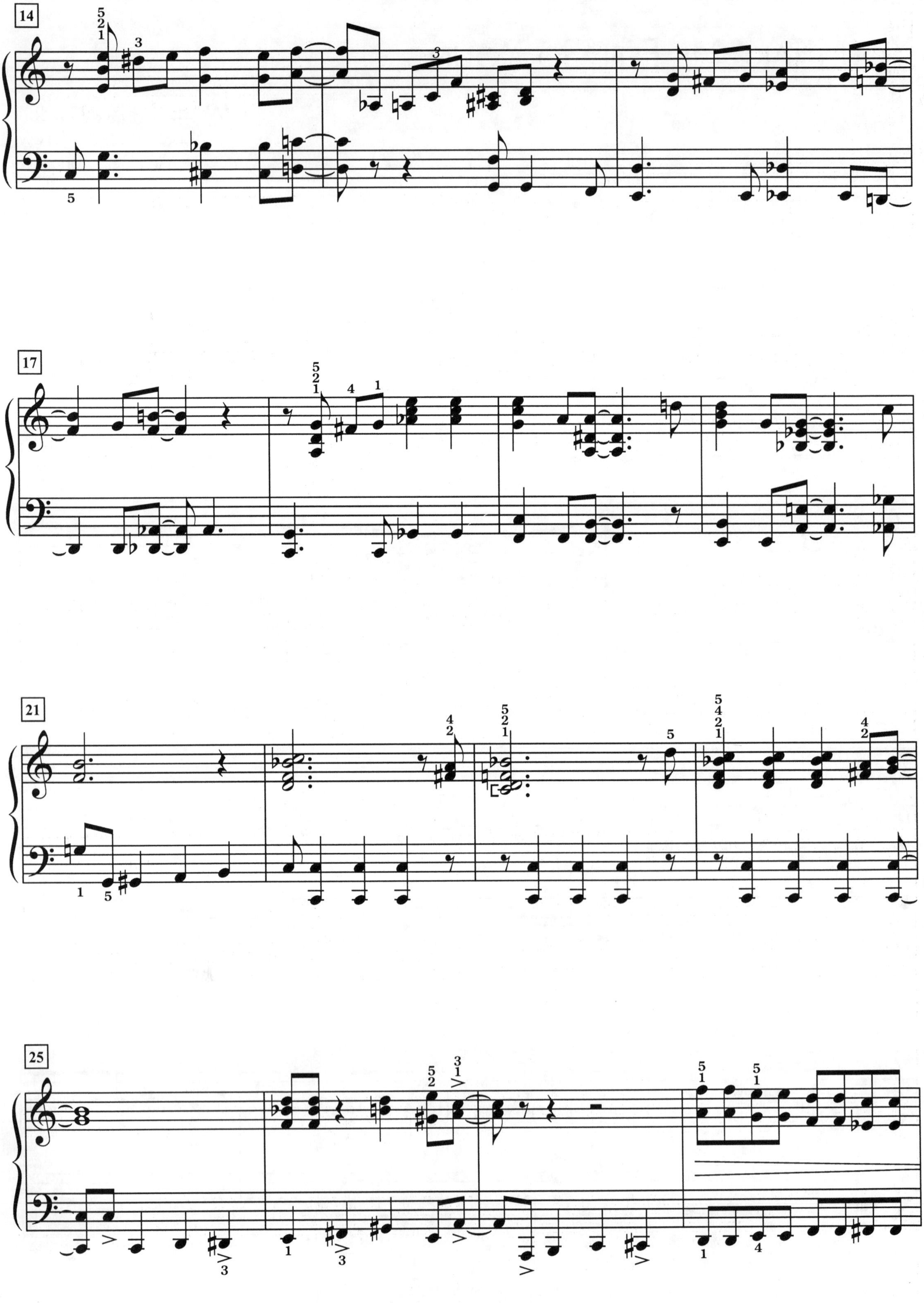
14
17
21
25

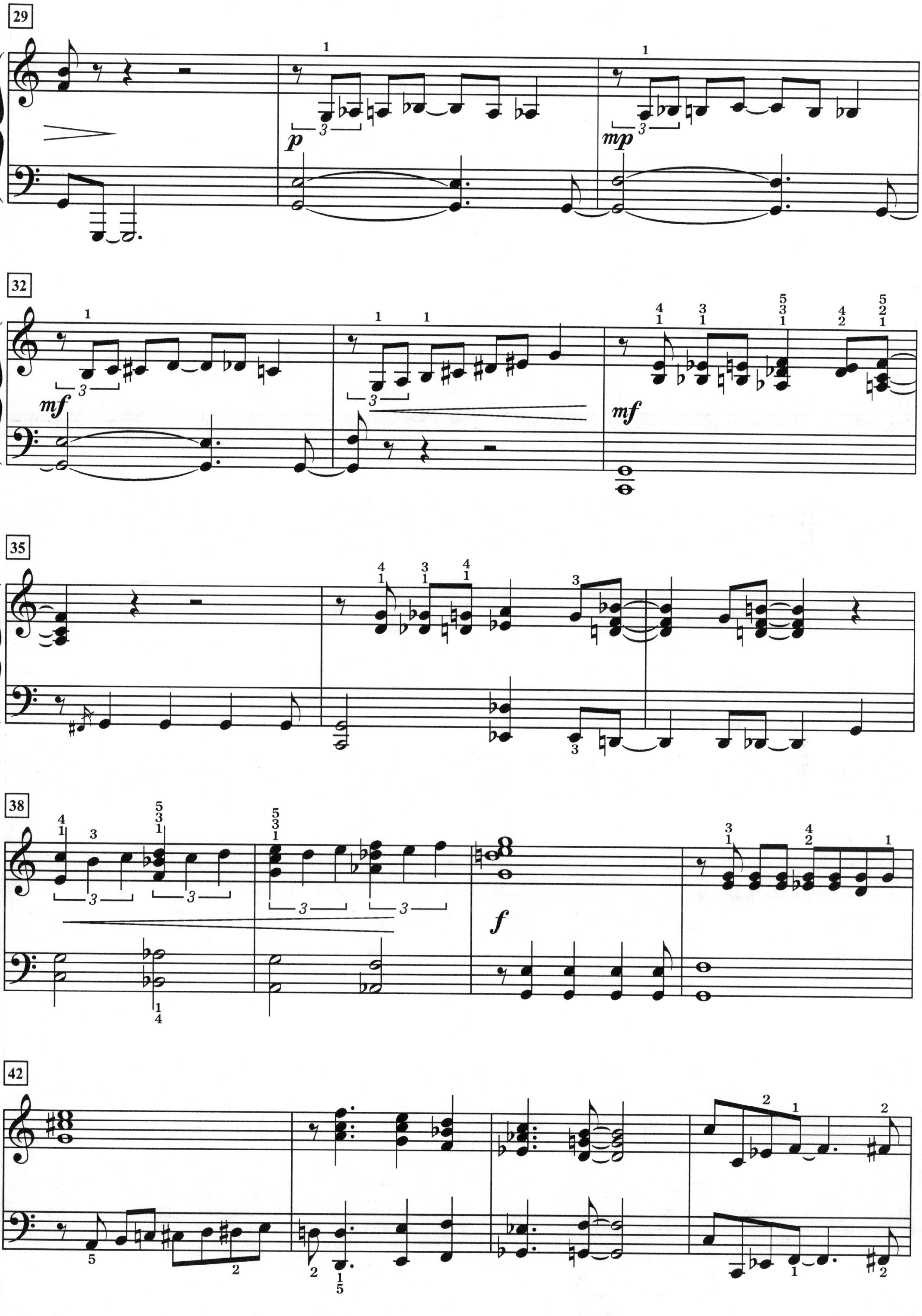
29
p
mp
32
mf
mf
35
38
f
42

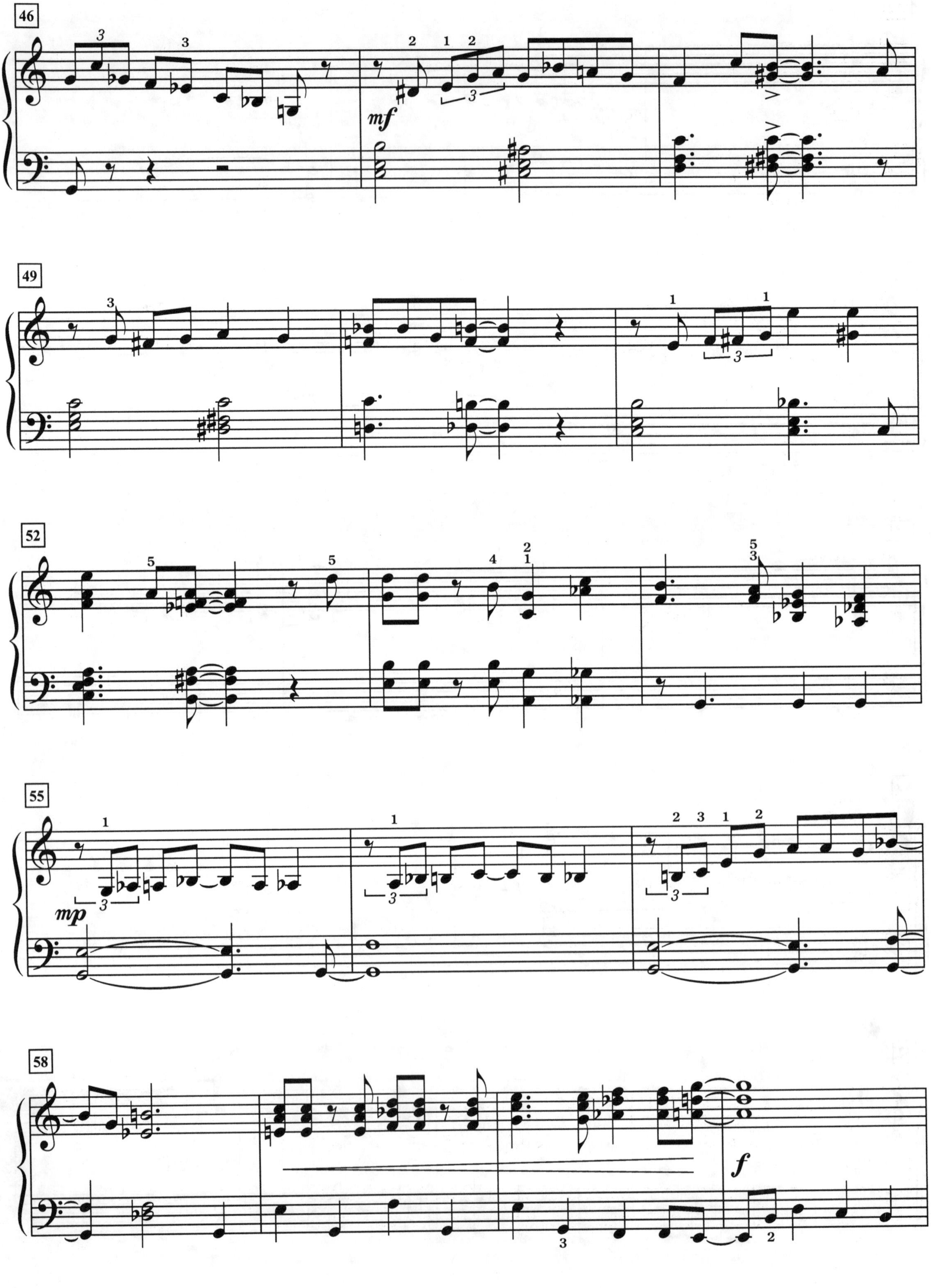
46
mf
49
52
55
mp
58
f

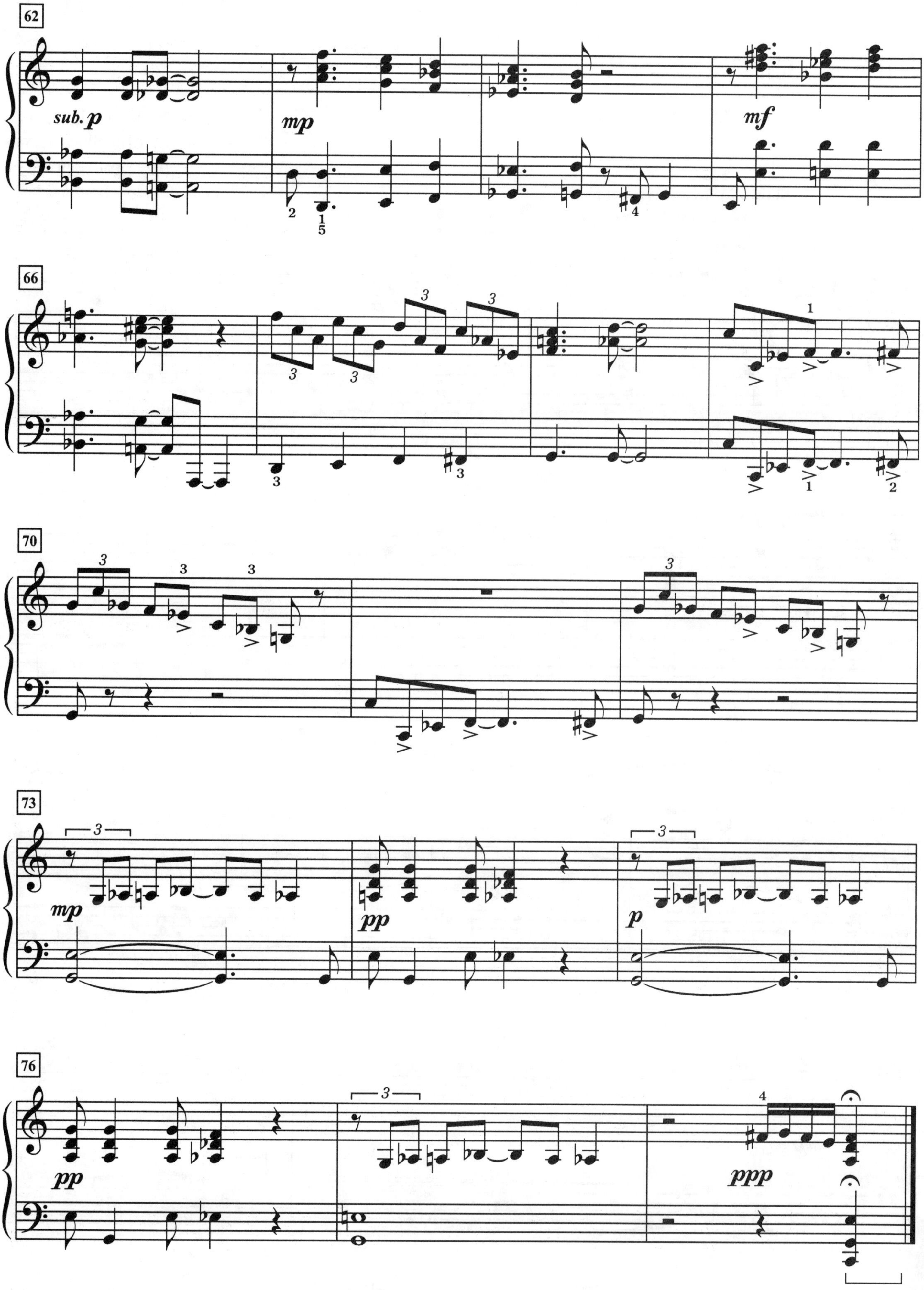
62
sub. p
mp
mf
66
70
73
mp
pp
p
76
pp
ppp

Moonlight in Vermont

Music by Karl Suessdorf
Lyric by John Blackburn
Arr. Bert Konowitz

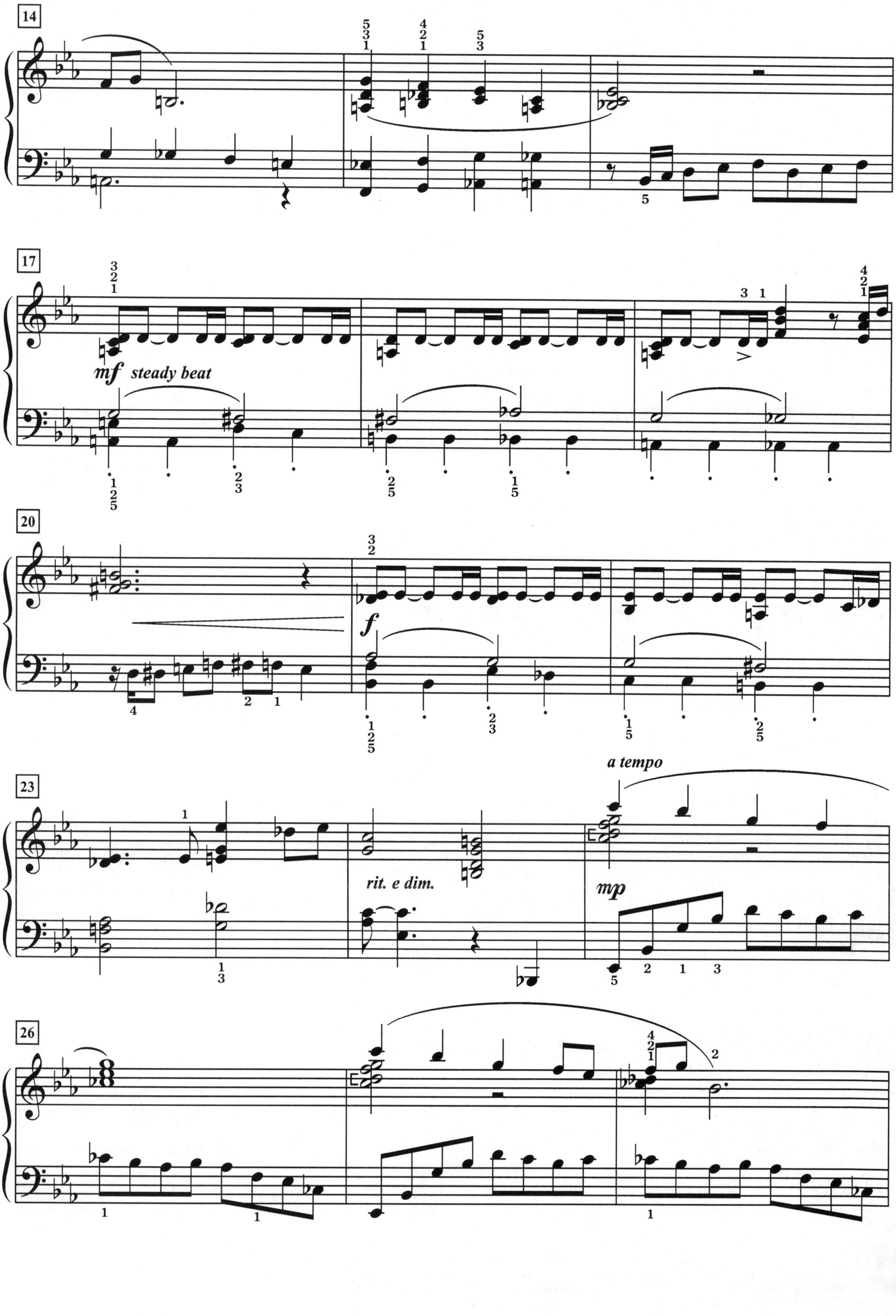
14
17
mf steady beat
20
f
23
a tempo
rit. e dim.
mp
26

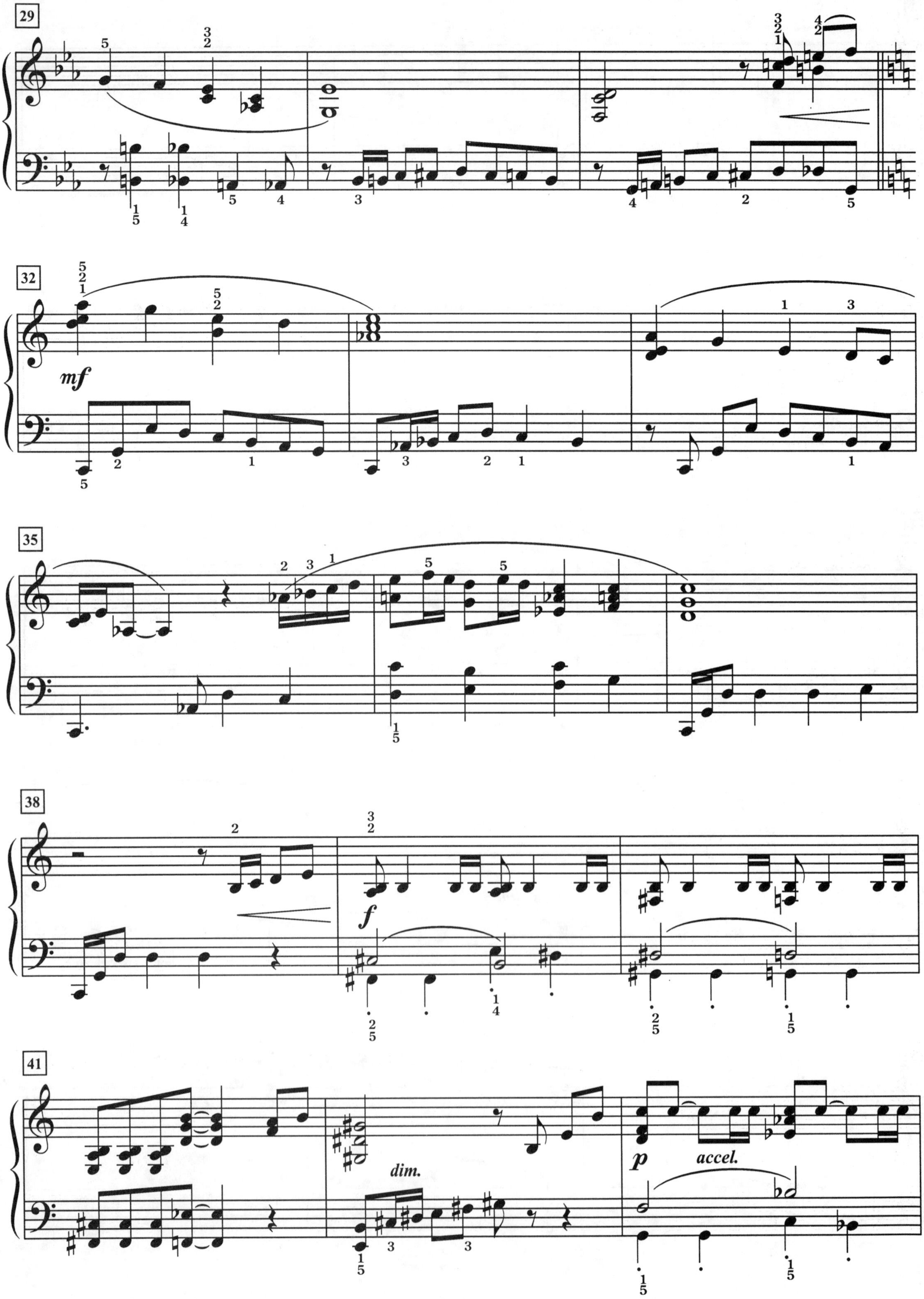
29
32
mf
35
38
f
41
dim.
p
accel.

44
cresc. e rit.
47
a tempo
mf
50
p
53
mf
p
rit. e dim.
56
molto rit.
very slowly
ppp

My Foolish Heart

Words by Ned Washington
Music by Victor Young
Arr. Bert Konowitz

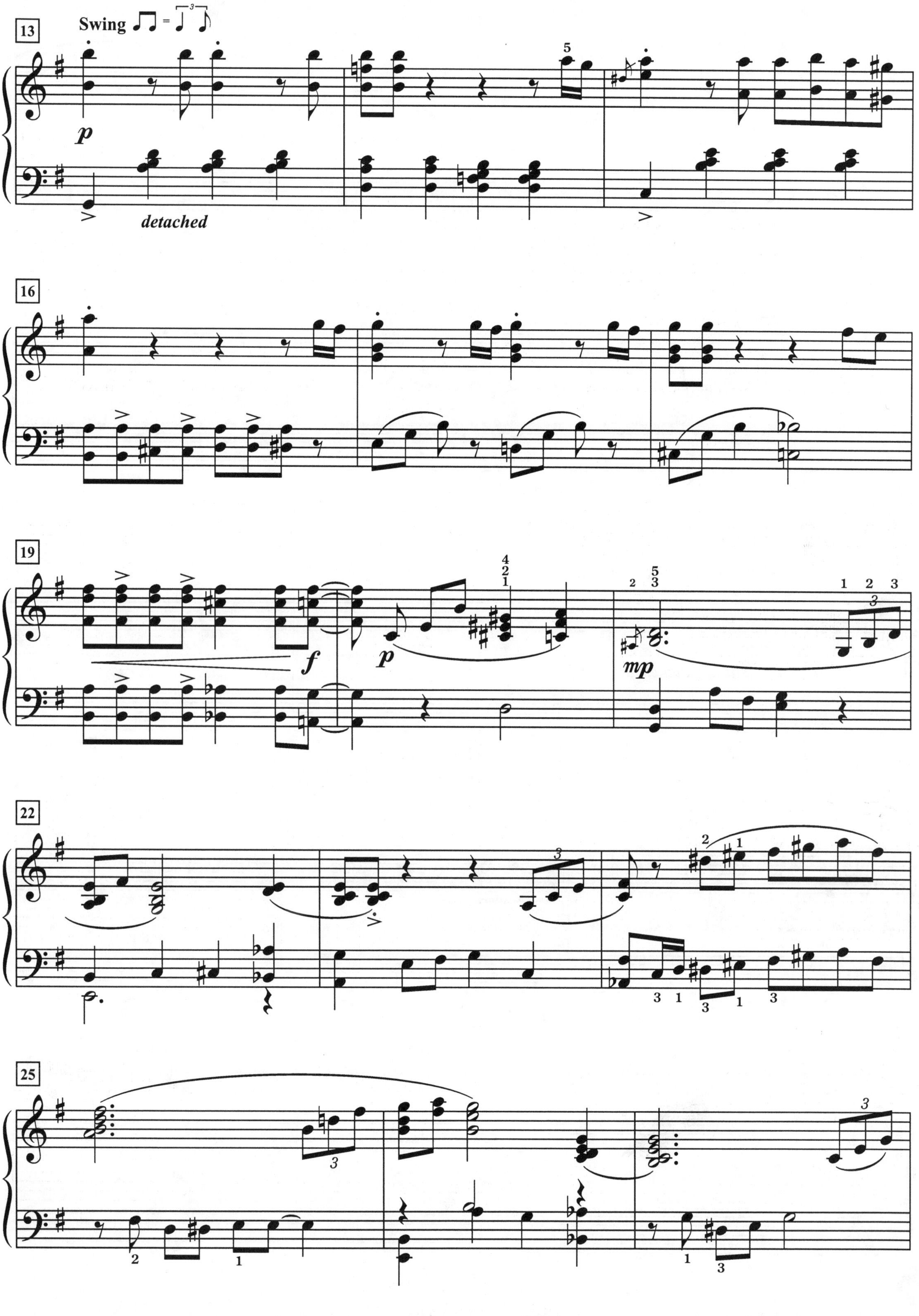
13
Swing
detached
16
19
22
25

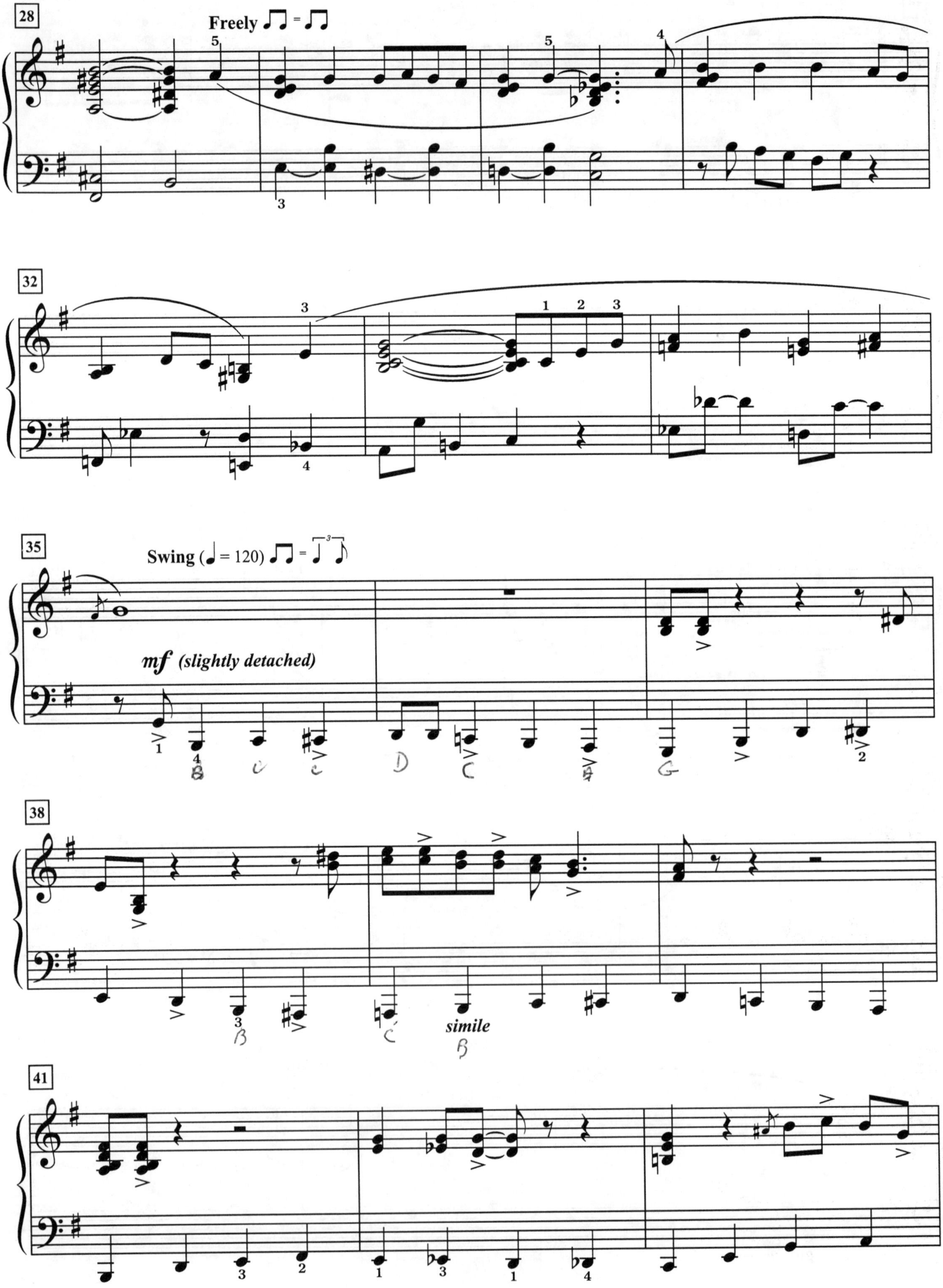
28
Freely
32
35
Swing (♩ = 120)
mf (slightly detached)
38
simile
41

44
Freely ♫ = ♫
mp
47
p
50
a tempo (♩= 96)
rit.
53
rit. e dim.
56
pp
very slow and deliberate

You'll Never Know

Lyrics by Mack Gordon
Music by Harry Warren
Arr. Bert Konowitz

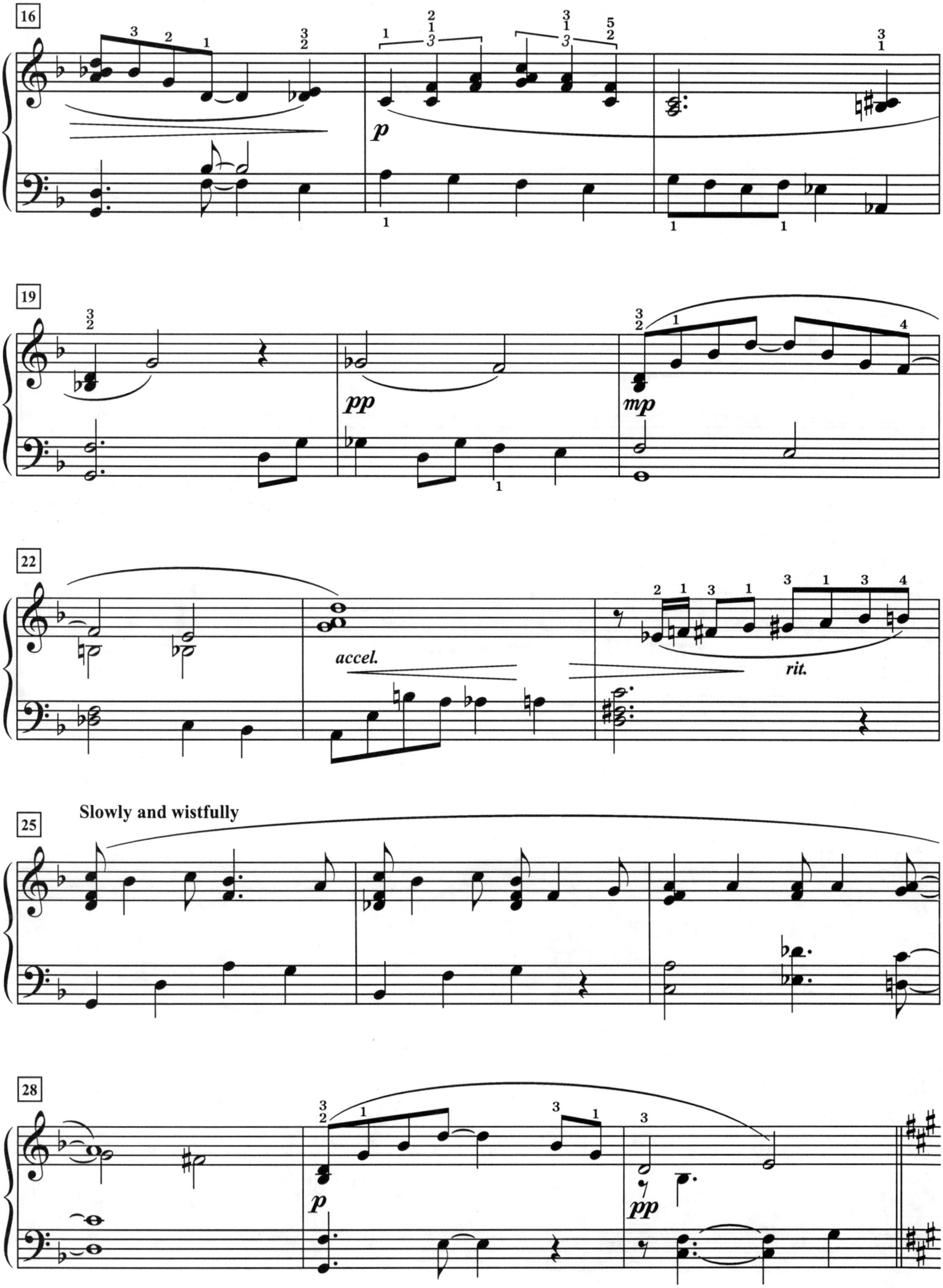
16
p
19
pp
mp
22
accel.
rit.
25
Slowly and wistfully
28
p
pp

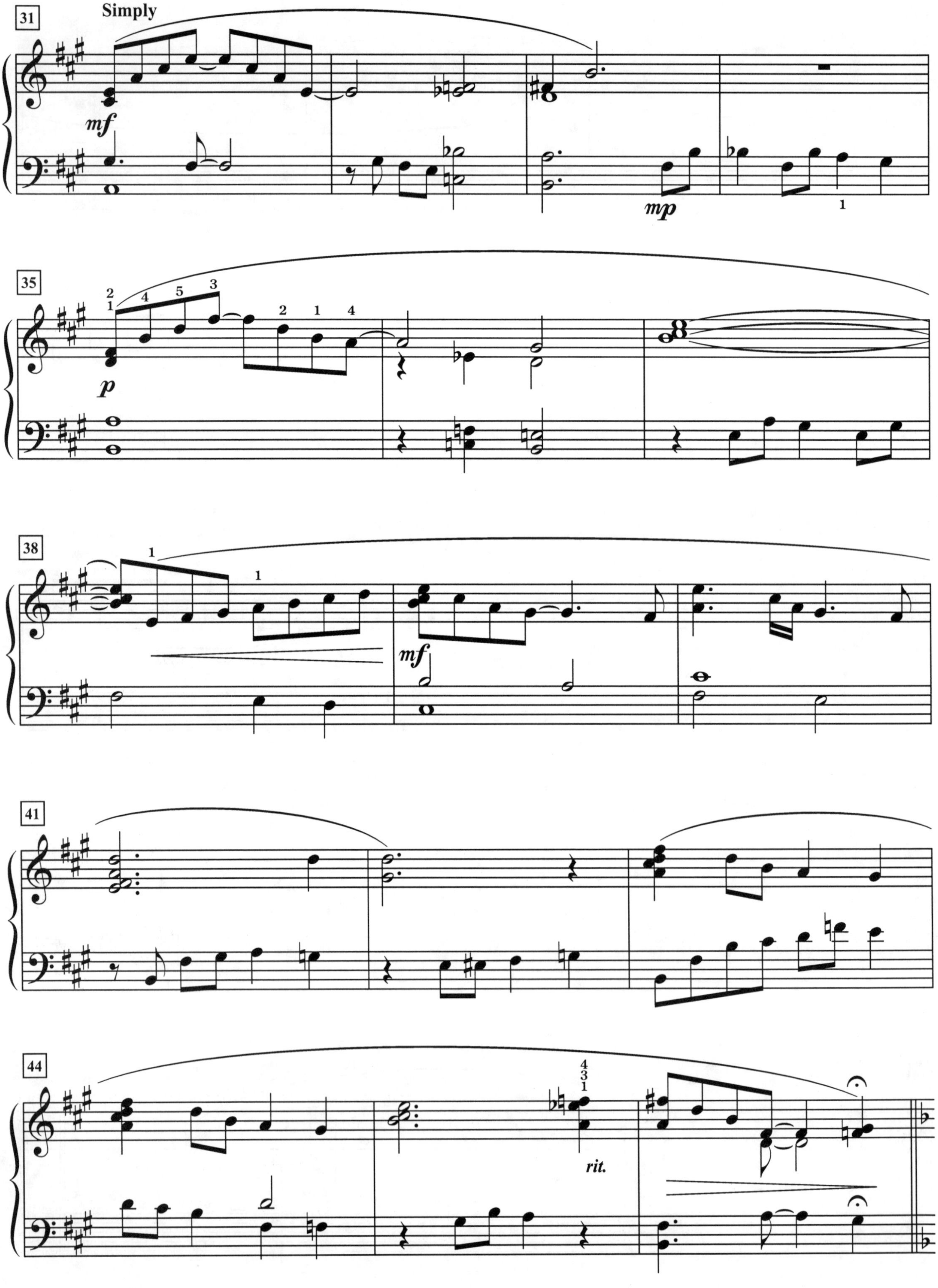
31
Simply
mf
mp
35
p
38
mf
41
44
rit.

47
a tempo
pp distantly
mp
51
p
accel.
rit.
Slowly and wistfully
55
59
p
pp
63
p
rit.
Slowly
pp